God's Little Instruction Book
for the Class of 2000

Honor Books
Tulsa, Oklahoma

God's Little Instruction Book for the Class of 2000
ISBN 1-56292-648-9
Copyright © 2000 by Honor Books
P. O. Box 55388
Tulsa, Oklahoma 74155

Script compiled by M. Allaby, Florissant, Colorado.

INTRODUCTION

Congratulations! As a member of the Class of 2000, you are being launched into the world at one of the most exciting times in recorded history. Speculation abounds, anticipation builds. There is talk of a sparkling new millennium filled with intergalactic exploration and the advancement of new and astounding technologies. What a time to be alive!

At the same time, our world now seems to be a much more challenging and daunting place to live. How do you make good choices when everything around you is moving and changing at breakneck speed? And how do you cut through the hype and determine what's best for your life?

In *God's Little Instruction Book for the Class of 2000*, we at Honor Books offer you insight and wisdom fit for a new millennium. We hope the timeless truths presented in these pages will help you build your life on a firm foundation and make a name for yourself in a new and exciting world filled with limitless possibilities.

YOU MAY LAUGH OUT LOUD IN THE FUTURE AT SOMETHING YOU'RE EATING YOUR HEART OUT OVER TODAY.

For our light affliction, which is but for a moment, worketh
for us a far more exceeding and eternal weight of glory.
2 Corinthians 4:17 KJV

THE PERSON WHO KNOWS "HOW" WILL ALWAYS HAVE A JOB. THE PERSON WHO KNOWS "WHY" WILL ALWAYS BE HIS BOSS.

How much better to get wisdom than gold! And to get understanding is to be chosen rather than silver.

Proverbs 16:16 NKJV

5

NEVER ALLOW YOUR SENSE OF SELF TO BECOME ASSOCIATED WITH YOUR SENSE OF JOB. IF YOUR JOB VANISHES, YOUR SELF DOESN'T.

What advantage does man have in all his work which he does under the sun? A generation goes and a generation comes, but the earth remains forever.

Ecclesiastes 1:3-4 NASB

6

CLASS OF 2000

COURAGE IS GRACE UNDER PRESSURE.

*We have this hope as an anchor for
the soul, firm and secure.*

Hebrews 6:19

ANXIETY DOES NOT EMPTY TOMORROW OF ITS SORROWS, BUT ONLY EMPTIES TODAY OF ITS STRENGTH.

Cast your cares on the LORD and he will sustain you.
Psalm 55:22

IT'S ONLY POSSIBLE TO LIVE HAPPILY EVER AFTER ON A DAY-TO-DAY BASIS.

So don't be anxious about tomorrow. God will take care of your tomorrow too. Live one day at a time.

Matthew 6:34 TLB

9

ALWAYS DO RIGHT. THIS WILL GRATIFY SOME AND ASTONISH THE REST.

I want you to stress these things, so that those who have trusted in God may be careful to devote themselves to doing what is good. These things are excellent and profitable for everyone.

Titus 3:8

WHAT COUNTS IS NOT THE NUMBER OF HOURS YOU PUT IN, BUT HOW MUCH YOU PUT IN THE HOURS.

Therefore be careful how you walk, not as unwise men,
but as wise, making the most of your time,
because the days are evil.
Ephesians 5:15-16 NASB

SMART IS BELIEVING HALF OF WHAT YOU HEAR; BRILLIANT IS KNOWING WHICH HALF TO BELIEVE.

*For wisdom and truth will enter the very center
of your being, filling your life with joy.*

Proverbs 2:10 TLB

12

EVERYTHING THAT IS DONE IN THE WORLD IS DONE BY HOPE.

Find rest, O my soul, in God alone;
my hope comes from him.

Psalm 62:5

THERE'S ONLY ONE CORNER OF THE UNIVERSE YOU CAN BE CERTAIN OF IMPROVING, AND THAT'S YOUR OWN SELF.

Hold on to instruction, do not let it go;
guard it well, for it is your life.

Proverbs 4:13

God's Little Instruction Book

TODAY IS THE TOMORROW WE WORRIED ABOUT YESTERDAY.

*Will all your worries add a single
moment to your life?*

Matthew 6:27 TLB

15

God's Little Instruction Book

NOTHING IS WORTH MORE THAN THIS DAY.

The day is yours, and yours also the night;
you established the sun and moon.

Psalm 74:16

IDENTIFY YOUR HIGHEST SKILL AND DEVOTE YOUR TIME TO PERFORMING IT.

*Give diligence to make your calling and election sure,
for if ye do these things, ye shall never fall.*
2 Peter 1:10 KJV

17

GENIUS IS 1 PERCENT INSPIRATION AND 99 PERCENT PERSPIRATION.

For just as the body without the spirit is dead,
so also faith without works is dead.

James 2:26 NASB

18

EVERY MAN DIES; NOT EVERY MAN LIVES.

I came that they may have life, and have it abundantly!
John 10:10 NASB

IT IS THE PART OF A WISE MAN TO KEEP HIMSELF TODAY FOR TOMORROW, AND NOT TO VENTURE ALL HIS EGGS IN ONE BASKET.

It is not good to have zeal without knowledge,
nor to be hasty and miss the way.

Proverbs 19:2

20

THE ONLY THING WE HAVE TO FEAR IS FEAR ITSELF.

God is our refuge and strength, an ever-present help in trouble.
Therefore we will not fear.

Psalm 46:1-2

THE VALUE OF LIFE LIES NOT IN THE LENGTH OF DAYS, BUT IN THE USE WE MAKE OF THEM.

*Be very careful, then, how you live—not as unwise but as wise,
making the most of every opportunity.*

Ephesians 5:15-16

WHEN ONE DOOR CLOSES, ANOTHER DOOR OPENS.

Let your eyes look straight ahead,
fix your gaze directly before you.

Proverbs 4:25

WITH COURAGE YOU WILL
DARE TO TAKE RISKS,
HAVE THE STRENGTH TO BE
COMPASSIONATE AND THE
WISDOM TO BE HUMBLE.
COURAGE IS THE FOUNDATION
OF INTEGRITY.

Be on your guard; stand firm in the faith;
be men of courage; be strong. Do everything in love.
1 Corinthains 16:13-14

24

CLASS OF
2000

AH, BUT A MAN'S REACH SHOULD EXCEED HIS GRASP, OR WHAT'S HEAVEN FOR?

Now to him who is able to do immeasurably more than all we ask or imagine, according to his power that is at work within us.

Ephesians 3:20

EVERY OAK TREE STARTED OUT AS A COUPLE OF NUTS WHO STOOD THEIR GROUND.

Therefore, my dear brothers, stand firm. Let nothing move you.
Always give yourselves fully to the work of the Lord, because
you know that your labor in the Lord is not in vain.

1 Corinthians 15:58

CLASS OF 2000

WE MAKE A LIVING BY WHAT WE GET—WE MAKE A LIFE BY WHAT WE GIVE.

It is more blessed to give than to receive.

Acts 20:35 NASB

SLIGHT NOT WHAT'S NEAR THROUGH AIMING AT WHAT'S FAR.

*Do not boast about tomorrow, for you do not know
what a day may bring forth.*

Proverbs 27:1

28

IT IS A BLESSED THING THAT IN EVERY AGE SOMEONE HAS HAD ENOUGH INDIVIDUALITY AND COURAGE TO STAND BY HIS OWN CONVICTIONS.

Always be prepared to give an answer to everyone who asks you to give the reason for the hope that you have. But do this with gentleness and respect.

1 Peter 3:15

SELF CONTROL IS THE ABILITY TO KEEP COOL WHILE SOMEONE IS MAKING IT HOT FOR YOU.

A soft answer turns away wrath, but grievous words stir up anger.

Proverbs 15:1 AMP

30

God's Little Instruction Book

I TRY TO AVOID LOOKING FORWARD OR BACKWARD, AND TRY TO KEEP LOOKING UPWARD.

*I have set the LORD always before me. Because he is
at my right hand, I will not be shaken.*

Psalm 16:8

31

AVOIDING DANGER IS NO SAFER IN THE LONG RUN THAN OUTRIGHT EXPOSURE. LIFE IS EITHER A DARING ADVENTURE OR NOTHING.

I have told you these things, so that in me you may have peace. In this world you will have trouble. But take heart! I have overcome the world.

John 16:33

CLASS OF 2000

WHEN WE LONG FOR LIFE
WITHOUT DIFFICULTIES, REMIND
US THAT OAKS GROW STRONG IN
CONTRARY WINDS AND DIAMONDS
ARE MADE UNDER PRESSURE.

Perseverance must finish its work so that you may be
mature and complete, not lacking anything.
James 1:4

33

WHAT THE CATERPILLAR CALLS THE END OF THE WORLD THE MASTER CALLS A BUTTERFLY.

And we, who with unveiled faces all reflect the Lord's glory, are being transformed into his likeness with ever-increasing glory.

2 Corinthians 3:18

MOST OF THE IMPORTANT THINGS
IN THE WORLD HAVE BEEN
ACCOMPLISHED BY PEOPLE
WHO HAVE KEPT ON TRYING
WHEN THERE SEEMED
TO BE NO HOPE AT ALL.

*So now, go. I am sending you to Pharaoh to bring my people
the Israelites out of Egypt.*

Exodus 3:10

God's Little Instruction Book

HAVE COURAGE FOR THE GREAT
SORROWS OF LIFE AND PATIENCE
FOR THE SMALL ONES; AND WHEN
YOU HAVE LABORIOUSLY
ACCOMPLISHED YOUR DAILY TASK,
GO TO SLEEP IN PEACE.
GOD IS AWAKE.

He will not let your foot slip—he who watches over you will not slumber.
Psalm 121:3

CLASS OF
2000

PEOPLE MAY DOUBT WHAT YOU SAY, BUT THEY WILL BELIEVE WHAT YOU DO.

My little children, let us not love in word,
neither in tongue; but in deed and in truth.

1 John 3:18 KJV

37

WHEN YOU COME TO THE END OF YOUR ROPE . . . TIE A KNOT AND HANG ON.

Cast all your anxiety on him because he cares for you.
1 Peter 5:7

38

EVERY MYSTERY SOLVED BRINGS US TO THE THRESHOLD OF A GREATER ONE.

He has made everything beautiful in its time. He has also set eternity in the hearts of men; yet they cannot fathom what God has done from beginning to end.

Ecclesiastes 3:11

REAL KNOWLEDGE IS TO KNOW THE EXTENT OF ONE'S IGNORANCE.

But seek ye first the kingdom of God, and his righteousness;
and all these things shall be added unto you.

Matthew 6:33 KJV

40

THERE IS A NAME FOR PEOPLE WHO ARE NOT EXCITED ABOUT THEIR WORK—UNEMPLOYED.

Whatever you do, work at it with all your heart,
as working for the Lord, not for men.
Colossians 3:23

A SHIP IN HARBOR IS SAFE, BUT THAT IS NOT WHAT SHIPS ARE BUILT FOR.

You are the world's light—a city on a hill, glowing in the night for all to see. Don't hide your light!
Matthew 5:14-15 TLB

THE BEST BRIDGE BETWEEN HOPE AND DESPAIR IS OFTEN A GOOD NIGHT'S SLEEP.

It is vain for you to rise up early, to sit up late, to eat the bread of sorrows: for so he giveth his beloved sleep.

Psalm 127:2 KJV

TAKING SOMEONE'S TIME IS THE ONLY DEBT THAT CAN'T BE REPAID.

Teach us to number our days aright, that we
may gain a heart of wisdom.

Psalm 90:12

44

HOPE SPRINGS ETERNAL IN THE HUMAN HEART.

The LORD delights in those who fear him,
who put their hope in his unfailing love.

Psalm 147:11

45

THE WORLD IS GOVERNED MORE BY APPEARANCE THAN REALITIES.

These are a shadow of the things that were to come;
the reality, however, is found in Christ.

Colossians 2:17

A GOOD LAUGH IS SUNSHINE IN A HOUSE.

A cheerful heart is good medicine.

Proverbs 17:22

CLASS OF
2000

LIFE CAN ONLY BE UNDERSTOOD BACKWARDS; BUT IT MUST BE LIVED FORWARDS.

This is what the LORD says—your Redeemer, the Holy One of Israel:
"I am the LORD your God, who teaches you what is best for you,
who directs you in the way you should go."

Isaiah 48:17

HUMOR IS TO LIFE WHAT SHOCK ABSORBERS ARE TO AUTOMOBILES.

A merry heart doeth good like a medicine:
but a broken spirit drieth the bones.

Proverbs 17:22 KJV

49

SOME PEOPLE SUCCEED
BECAUSE THEY ARE DESTINED
TO, BUT MOST PEOPLE
SUCCEED BECAUSE THEY ARE
DETERMINED TO.

Having done all to stand ... Stand therefore.
Ephesians 6:13-14 KJV

CONTENTMENT IS DIRECTLY PROPORTIONATE TO THE MEASURE YOU GIVE OF YOURSELF.

Therefore, as we have opportunity, let us do good to all people.

Galatians 6:10

CLASS OF
2000

I THINK THE ONE LESSON I HAVE LEARNED IS THAT THERE IS NO SUBSTITUTE FOR PAYING ATTENTION.

Therefore we ought to give the more earnest heed to the things which we have heard, lest at any time we should let them slip.

Hebrews 2:1 KJV

CLASS OF
2000

DON'T ALLOW THE FUTURE TO SCARE YOU.

Whoever trusts in the LORD is kept safe.

Proverbs 29:25

KEEP TRYING TO WIN; KEEP PLAYING THE GAME; BUT KEEP ROOM IN YOUR HEART FOR A SONG.

He put a new song in my mouth, a hymn of praise to our God.
Psalm 40:3

54

THE GREATER PART OF OUR HAPPINESS DEPENDS ON OUR DISPOSITION AND NOT OUR CIRCUMSTANCES.

I know how to live on almost nothing or with everything. I have learned the secret of contentment in every situation.
Philippians 4:12 TLB

THE HAPPIEST PEOPLE ARE THOSE WHO DO THE MOST FOR OTHERS.

*Carry each other's burdens, and in this way
you will fulfill the law of Christ.*

Galations 6:2

56

TAKE TIME TO DELIBERATE;
BUT WHEN THE TIME FOR
ACTION ARRIVES, STOP
THINKING AND GO ON.

Rise up; this matter is in your hands. We will
support you, so take courage and do it.

Ezra 10:4

DO NOT BORROW TROUBLE BY DREADING TOMORROW. IT IS THE DARK MENACE OF THE FUTURE THAT MAKES COWARDS OF US ALL.

*For he will command his angels concerning you
to guard you in all your ways.*

Psalm 91:11

58

DON'T BE AFRAID OF PRESSURE. REMEMBER THAT PRESSURE IS WHAT TURNS A LUMP OF COAL INTO A DIAMOND.

Knowing this, that the trying of your faith worketh patience. But let patience have her perfect work, that ye may be perfect and entire, wanting nothing.
James 1: 3-4 KJV

59

SCHOOL SEEKS TO GET YOU READY FOR EXAMINATION; LIFE GIVES THE FINALS.

*Examine yourselves to see whether you
are in the faith: test yourselves.*

2 Corinthians 13:5

60

THINK OF THESE THINGS— WHENCE YOU CAME, WHERE YOU ARE GOING, AND TO WHOM YOU MUST ACCOUNT.

"I am the Alpha and the Omega," says the Lord God, "who is, and who was, and who is to come, the Almighty."

Revelation 1:8

CLASS OF
2000

WE LIVE IN DEEDS, NOT YEARS; IN
THOUGHTS, NOT BREATHS.
WE SHOULD COUNT TIME BY
HEARTTHROBS. HE MOST LIVES
WHO THINKS MOST—FEELS THE
NOBLEST—ACTS THE BEST.

*"For in him we live and move and have our being." As some of
your own poets have said, "We are his offspring."*

Acts 17:28

62

A TRUE FRIEND IS ONE SOUL IN TWO BODIES.

*Jonathan became one in spirit with David,
and he loved him as himself.*

1 Samuel 18:1

THE FUTURE BELONGS TO THOSE WHO BELIEVE IN THE BEAUTY OF THEIR DREAMS.

Anything is possible if you have faith.

Mark 9:23 TLB

CLASS OF
2000

NO PASSION SO EFFECTUALLY ROBS THE MIND OF ALL ITS POWERS OF ACTING AND REASONING AS FEAR.

You will keep in perfect peace him whose mind is steadfast, because he trusts in you.

Isaiah 26:3

NOT FARE WELL, BUT FARE FORWARD, VOYAGERS.

I am with you and will watch over you wherever you go.

Genesis 28:15

HAPPY IS HE WHO HAS BEEN ABLE TO LEARN THE CAUSES OF THINGS.

Those who are wise will shine like the brightness of the heavens.

Daniel 12:3

PEOPLE MAY DOUBT WHAT YOU SAY, BUT THEY WILL ALWAYS BELIEVE WHAT YOU DO.

For the tree is known and recognized and judged by its fruit.
Matthew 12:33 AMP

68

SEIZE TODAY, AND PUT AS LITTLE TRUST AS YOU CAN IN THE MORROW.

*Since no man knows the future, who can
tell him what is to come?*

Ecclesiastes 8:7

EVERY CALLING IS GREAT WHEN GREATLY PURSUED.

I press toward the mark for the prize of the high calling of God in Christ Jesus.

Philippians 3:14 KJV

70

THE MOST IMPORTANT SINGLE INGREDIENT IN THE FORMULA OF SUCCESS IS KNOWING HOW TO GET ALONG WITH PEOPLE.

See that no one pays back evil for evil, but always try to do good to each other and to everyone else.

1 Thessalonians 5:15 TLB

71

WHO FINDS A FAITHFUL FRIEND FINDS A TREASURE.

If one falls down, his friend can help him up. But pity the man who falls and has no one to help him up!

Ecclesiastes 4:10

PEOPLE MUST HELP ONE ANOTHER, IT'S NATURE'S LAW.

And do not forget to do good and to share with others,
for with such sacrifices God is pleased.

Hebrews 13:16

THE BIBLE HAS A WORD TO DESCRIBE "SAFE" SEX: IT'S CALLED MARRIAGE.

Marriage should be honored by all, and the marriage bed kept pure.
Hebrews 13:4

ONE MUST ALWAYS HAVE ONE'S BOOTS ON AND BE READY TO GO.

*You also must be ready, because the Son of Man will come
at an hour when you do not expect him.*

Luke 12:40

LOOK BACK AND SMILE AT PERILS PAST.

We know that in all things God works for the good of those who love him, who have been called according to his purpose.

Romans 8:28

SHOOT FOR THE MOON. EVEN IF YOU MISS, YOU WILL LAND AMONG THE STARS.

Aim for perfection.

2 Corinthians 13:11

77

HASTEN SLOWLY.

But if from there you seek the LORD your God,
you will find him if you look for him
with all your heart and with all your soul.
                                    Deuteronomy 4:29

OUT OF DEBT, OUT OF DANGER.

Give everyone what you owe him....
Let no debt remain outstanding.

Romans 13:7-8

THE SECRET OF SUCCESS IS TO DO THE COMMON THINGS UNCOMMONLY WELL.

Seest thou a man diligent in his business? He shall stand before kings; he shall not stand before mean men.
Proverbs 22:29 KJV

80

God's Little Instruction Book

I'VE SUFFERED A GREAT MANY CATASTROPHES IN MY LIFE. MOST OF THEM NEVER HAPPENED.

I will lie down and sleep in peace, for you alone,
O LORD, make me dwell in safety.

Psalm 4:8

81

YOU ARE ONLY WHAT YOU ARE WHEN NO ONE IS LOOKING.

Not with eyeservice as menpleasers; but as the servants of Christ, doing the will of God from the heart.
Ephesians 6:6 KJV

82

God's Little Instruction Book

IF PEACE BE IN THE HEART, THE WILDEST WINTER STORM IS FULL OF SOLEMN BEAUTY.

And the peace of God, which transcends all understanding,
will guard your hearts and your minds in Christ Jesus.
Philippians 4:7

83

ALL THE WAY MY SAVIOR LEADS ME;
WHAT HAVE I TO ASK BESIDE?
CAN I DOUBT HIS TENDER MERCY,
WHO THROUGH LIFE
HAS BEEN MY GUIDE?

For this God is our God for ever and ever;
he will be our guide even to the end.

Psalm 48:14

84

LOVE IS PRESSING AROUND US ON ALL SIDES LIKE AIR. CEASE TO RESIST IT AND INSTANTLY LOVE TAKES POSSESSION.

This is love: not that we loved God, but that he loved us and sent his Son as an atoning sacrifice for our sins.

1 John 4:10

YOU CAN LEAD A BOY TO COLLEGE, BUT YOU CANNOT MAKE HIM THINK.

It is senseless to pay tuition to educate a
rebel who has no heart for truth.

Proverbs 17:16 TLB

86

THE BEST THINGS ARE NEAREST:
BREATH IN YOUR NOSTRILS, LIGHT
IN YOUR EYES, FLOWERS AT YOUR
FEET, DUTIES AT YOUR HAND, THE
PATH OF GOD JUST BEFORE YOU.

Give thanks to the LORD, for he is good;
his love endures forever.

1 Chronicles 16:34

87

God's Little Instruction Book

THE BEST THINGS IN LIFE ARE NOT FREE.

Forasmuch as ye know that ye were not redeemed with corruptible things,
as silver and gold ... but with the precious blood of Christ,
as of a lamb without blemish and without spot.

1 Peter 1:18-19 KJV

OPPORTUNITIES ARE SELDOM LABELED.

*Seek and ye shall find; knock, and it
shall be opened unto you.*

Matthew 7:7 KJV

AN INFINITE GOD CAN GIVE ALL OF HIMSELF TO EACH OF HIS CHILDREN . . . TO EACH ONE HE GIVES ALL OF HIMSELF AS FULLY AS IF THERE WERE NO OTHERS.

The LORD appeared to us in the past, saying: "I have loved you with an everlasting love; I have drawn you with loving-kindness."
Jeremiah 31:3

90

BLESSED IS THE MAN WHO FINDS OUT WHICH WAY GOD IS MOVING AND THEN GETS GOING IN THE SAME DIRECTION.

Whether you turn to the right or to the left, your ears will hear a voice behind you, saying, "This is the way; walk in it."

Isaiah 30:21

91

NOTHING GREAT WAS EVER ACHIEVED WITHOUT ENTHUSIASM.

For the joy of the Lord is your strength.

Nehemiah 8:10

92

DEBT IS
THE WORST
POVERTY.

The borrower is servant to the lender.

Proverbs 22:7

93

THE BEST THING ABOUT THE FUTURE IS THAT IT COMES ONLY ONE DAY AT A TIME.

We are being renewed day by day.
2 Corinthians 4:16

94

THE FUTURE LIES BEFORE YOU,
LIKE PATHS OF PURE WHITE
SNOW. BE CAREFUL HOW
YOU TREAD IT, FOR EVERY
STEP WILL SHOW.

*In everything you do, put God first, and he will
direct you and crown your efforts with success.*

Proverbs 3:6 TLB

95

FEAR DEFEATS MORE PEOPLE THAN ANY OTHER ONE THING IN THE WORLD.

Perfect love drives out fear.

1 John 4:18

MATURITY DOESN'T COME WITH AGE; IT COMES WITH ACCEPTANCE OF RESPONSIBILITY.

When I was a child, I spake as a child, I understood as a child, I thought as a child; but when I became a man, I put away childish things.
1 Corinthians 13:11 KJV

LEARN BY EXPERIENCE— PREFERABLY OTHER PEOPLE'S.

All these things happened to them as examples—as object lessons to us—
to warn us against doing the same things.
1 Corinthians 10:11 TLB

NEVER FEAR SHADOWS. THEY SIMPLY MEAN THERE'S A LIGHT SHINING SOMEWHERE NEARBY.

O Lord, you are my light!
You make my darkness bright.
2 Samuel 22:29 TLB

CLASS OF 2000

CONQUER YOURSELF RATHER THAN THE WORLD.

*Similarly, encourage the young men
to be self-controlled.*

Titus 2:6

GIVE YOUR PROBLEMS TO GOD; HE WILL BE UP ALL NIGHT ANYWAY.

And even the very hairs of your head are all numbered.
So don't be afraid; you are worth more than many sparrows.

Matthew 10:30-31

CLASS OF 2000

TO LOVE WHAT YOU DO AND FEEL THAT IT MATTERS —HOW COULD ANYTHING BE MORE FUN?

For my heart rejoiced in all my labour.
Ecclesiastes 2:10 KJV

102

CAST YOUR CARES ON GOD; THAT ANCHOR HOLDS.

*I will say of the LORD, "He is my refuge
and my fortress, my God, in whom I trust."*

Psalm 91:2

CLASS OF
2000

103

THE FUTURE BELONGS TO THOSE WHO SEE POSSIBILITIES BEFORE THEY BECOME OBVIOUS.

For the vision is yet for an appointed time ...
it will surely come, it will not tarry.

Habakkuk 2:3 KJV

104

God's Little Instruction Book

THE IDEAL MAN BEARS THE
ACCIDENTS OF LIFE WITH
DIGNITY AND GRACE, MAKING
THE BEST OF CIRCUMSTANCES.

Give thanks in all circumstances, for this is
God's will for you in Christ Jesus.
1 Thessalonians 5:18

ACT BOLDLY AND UNSEEN FORCES WILL COME TO YOUR AID.

We have the Lord our God to
fight our battles for us!
2 Chronicles 32:8 *TLB*

106

COURAGE IS THE POWER TO LET GO OF THE FAMILIAR.

The LORD is the stronghold of my life—
of whom shall I be afraid?

Psalm 27:1

CLASS OF
2000

107

CARVE YOUR NAME ON HEARTS AND NOT ON MARBLE.

The only letter I need is you yourselves! They can see that you are a letter from Christ written by us ... not one carved on stone, but in human hearts.

2 Corinthians 3:2-3 TLB

THE DIFFERENCE BETWEEN ORDINARY AND EXTRAORDINARY IS THAT LITTLE EXTRA EFFORT.

Whatsoever thy hand findeth to do, do it with thy might.
Ecclesiastes 9:10 KJV

CLASS OF
2000

109

LIVE AS BRAVE MEN AND FACE ADVERSITY WITH STOUT HEARTS.

Rise up; this matter is in your hands. We will support you,
so take courage and do it.

Ezra 10:4

God's Little Instruction Book

IS HE ALONE WHO HAS COURAGE ON HIS RIGHT HAND AND FAITH ON HIS LEFT HAND?

He does not fear bad news, nor live in dread of what may happen.
For he is settled in his mind that Jehovah will take care of him.

Psalm 112:7 TLB

CLASS OF 2000

THE SECRET OF SUCCESS IS TO BE LIKE A DUCK— SMOOTH AND UNRUFFLED ON TOP, BUT PADDLING FURIOUSLY UNDERNEATH.

I laboured more abundantly than they all:
yet not I, but the grace of God which was with me.
1 Corinthians 15:10 KJV

112

STAND UPRIGHT, SPEAK THY
THOUGHTS, DECLARE THE
TRUTH THOU HAST, THAT ALL
MAY SHARE; BE BOLD,
PROCLAIM IT EVERYWHERE:
THEY ONLY LIVE WHO DARE.

*Speaking the truth in love, we will in all things grow up
into him who is the Head, that is, Christ.*

Ephesians 4:15

113

THE BURDEN WHICH IS WELL BORNE BECOMES LIGHT.

Carry each other's burdens, and in this way you will fulfill the law of Christ.

Galatians 6:2

114

MONEY IS A GOOD SERVANT BUT A BAD MASTER.

The rich ruleth over the poor, and the
borrower is servant to the lender.

Proverbs 22:7

COURAGE IS NOT THE ABSENCE OF FEAR, BUT RATHER THE JUDGMENT THAT SOMETHING ELSE IS MORE IMPORTANT THAN FEAR.

For Christ's love compels us, because we are convinced that one died for all.

2 Corinthians 5:14

IT IS AMIDST GREAT PERILS THAT WE SEE BRAVE HEARTS.

I will not fear the tens of thousands
drawn up against me on every side.

Psalm 3:6

MOST OF THE THINGS WORTH DOING IN THE WORLD HAD BEEN DECLARED IMPOSSIBLE BEFORE THEY WERE DONE.

With God all things are possible.
Matthew 19:26 KJV

118

WE ARE MADE STRONG BY THE DIFFICULTIES WE FACE, NOT BY THOSE WE EVADE.

In all these things we are more than conquerors
through him who loved us.

Romans 8:37

God's Little Instruction Book

THIS WORLD BELONGS TO THE MAN WHO IS WISE ENOUGH TO CHANGE HIS MIND IN THE PRESENCE OF FACTS.

Whoever heeds correction gains understanding.
Proverbs 15:32

120

DON'T COUNT ON YOUR EDUCATION TO MAKE YOU WISE.

He who trusts in himself is a fool,
but he who walks in wisdom is kept safe.
Proverbs 28:26

121

DON'T FEAR CHANGE— EMBRACE IT.

I am leaving you with a gift—peace of mind and heart!
And the peace I give isn't fragile like the peace
the world gives. So don't be troubled or afraid.

John 14:27 TLB

CALL ON GOD, BUT ROW AWAY FROM THE ROCKS.

Wisdom and good judgment live together,
for wisdom knows where to discover
knowledge and understanding.

Proverbs 8:12 TLB

NOTHING I CAN DO WILL CHANGE
THE STRUCTURE OF THE UNIVERSE.
BUT MAYBE, BY RAISING MY VOICE
I CAN HELP THE GREATEST OF ALL
CAUSES—GOODWILL AMONG MEN
AND PEACE ON EARTH.

Blessed are the peacemakers, for they will be called sons of God.
Matthew 5:9

124

VISION IS THE WORLD'S MOST DESPERATE NEED. THERE ARE NO HOPELESS SITUATIONS, ONLY PEOPLE WHO THINK HOPELESSLY.

Where there is no vision, the people perish.
Proverbs 29:18 KJV

125

PEOPLE DO NOT CHANGE WITH THE TIMES, THEY CHANGE THE TIMES.

*Take up your positions; stand firm and see
the deliverance the LORD will give you.*
2 Chronicles 20:17

126

A MAN CAN DO ANYTHING HE WANTS TO DO IN THIS WORLD, AT LEAST IF HE WANTS TO DO IT BADLY ENOUGH.

*I can do everything through him
who gives me strength.*

Philippians 4:13

MY JOB IS TO TAKE CARE OF THE POSSIBLE AND TRUST GOD WITH THE IMPOSSIBLE.

And they that know thy name will put their trust in thee:
for thou, Lord, hast not forsaken them that seek thee.
Psalm 9:10 KJV

THE STARS ARE CONSTANTLY SHINING, BUT OFTEN WE DO NOT SEE THEM UNTIL THE DARK HOURS.

God is our refuge and strength, an ever-present help in trouble.

Psalms 46:1

A PROFESSIONAL IS SOMEONE WHO CAN DO HIS BEST WORK WHEN HE DOESN'T FEEL LIKE IT.

*To win the contest you must deny yourselves many
things that would keep you from doing your best.*
1 Corinthians 9:25 TLB

CHRISTIAN, SEEK NOT YET REPOSE,
HEAR THY GUARDIAN ANGEL SAY,
"THOUGH ARE IN THE
MIDST OF FOES:
WATCH AND PRAY."

Be on your guard; stand firm in the faith;
be men of courage; be strong. Do everything in love.
1 Corinthians 16:13

131

EVERY TOMORROW HAS TWO HANDLES. WE CAN TAKE HOLD OF IT BY THE HANDLE OF ANXIETY, OR BY THE HANDLE OF FAITH.

Cast all your anxiety of him because he cares for you.
1 Peter 5:7

132

FAITH IS LIKE ELECTRICITY. YOU CAN'T SEE IT, BUT YOU CAN SEE THE LIGHT.

*Now faith is being sure of what we hope for
and certain of what we do not see.*

Hebrews 11:1

133

CLASS OF 2000

LEARN FROM YESTERDAY, LIVE FOR TODAY, HOPE FOR TOMORROW.

*We have this hope as an anchor for
the soul, firm and secure.*

Hebrews 6:19

134

BE AN OPTIMIST—AT LEAST UNTIL THEY START MOVING ANIMALS IN PAIRS TO CAPE CANAVERAL.

There is surely a future hope for you,
and your hope will not be cut off.

Proverbs 23:18

135

THERE ARE AT LEAST FOUR THINGS YOU CAN DO WITH YOUR HANDS. YOU CAN WRING THEM IN DESPAIR; FOLD THEM IN IDLENESS; CLENCH THEM IN ANGER; OR USE THEM TO HELP SOMEONE.

She opens her arms to the poor and extends her hands to the needy.
Proverbs 31:20

136

BEWARE OF THE HALF TRUTH. YOU MAY HAVE GOTTEN HOLD OF THE WRONG HALF.

So give your servant a discerning heart.

1 Kings 3:9

EVEN A MOSQUITO DOESN'T GET A SLAP ON THE BACK UNTIL IT STARTS TO WORK.

*Work hard so God can say to you, "Well done." Be a good workman,
one who does not need to be ashamed when God examines your work.*
                                        2 Timothy 2:15 TLB

138

CLASS OF
2000

NEVER BE AFRAID TO TRUST AN UNKNOWN FUTURE TO A KNOWN GOD.

I will turn the darkness into light before them
and make the rough places smooth.

Isaiah 42:16

THE FUTURE IS AS BRIGHT AS THE PROMISES OF GOD.

For no matter how many promises God has made, they are "Yes" in Christ.

2 Corinthians 1:20

WHERE FEAR IS PRESENT, WISDOM CANNOT BE.

The LORD is my light and my salvation—whom shall I fear?

Psalm 27:1

THE ONLY PREPARATION FOR TOMORROW IS THE RIGHT USE OF TODAY.

Take therefore no thought for the morrow: for the morrow shall take thought for the things of itself. Sufficient unto the day is the evil thereof.

Matthew 6:34 KJV

142

WHEN I DESPAIR, I REMEMBER THAT ALL THROUGH HISTORY THE WAY OF TRUTH AND LOVE HAS ALWAYS WON.

The Lord knows how to rescue godly men from trials.
2 Peter 2:9

143

DO NOT FOLLOW WHERE THE PATH MAY LEAD. GO INSTEAD WHERE THERE IS NO PATH AND LEAVE A TRAIL.

Your ears shall hear a word behind you,
saying, "This is the way, walk in it."
Isaiah 30:21 NKJV

HE WHO WANTS MILK SHOULD NOT SIT ON A STOOL IN THE MIDDLE OF THE PASTURE EXPECTING THE COW TO BACK UP TO HIM.

Lazy hands make a man poor, but diligent hands bring wealth.

Proverbs 10:4

TO US ALSO, THROUGH EVERY
STAR, THROUGH EVERY BLADE
OF GRASS, IS NOT GOD MADE
VISIBLE IF WE WILL OPEN OUR
MINDS AND OUR EYES.

*The heavens declare the glory of God; the skies
proclaim the work of his hands.*

Psalm 19:1

146

BELIEVE IN LIFE.

You have made known to me the path of life;
you will fill me with joy in your presence.

Psalms 16:11

CLASS OF
2000

147

THE HAPPIEST PEOPLE DON'T NECESSARILY HAVE THE BEST OF EVERYTHING. THEY JUST MAKE THE BEST OF EVERYTHING.

For I have learned to be content whatever the circumstances.

Philippians 4:11

148

BECOME SO WRAPPED UP IN SOMETHING YOU FORGET TO BE AFRAID.

*So our aim is to please him always
in everything we do.*
2 Corinthians 5:9 TLB

BEING AT PEACE WITH YOURSELF IS A DIRECT RESULT OF FINDING PEACE WITH GOD.

And the peace of God, which passeth all understanding,
shall keep your hearts and minds through Christ Jesus.
Philippians 4:7 KJV

God's Little Instruction Book

OUR DOUBTS ARE TRAITORS AND MAKE US LOSE THE GOOD WE MIGHT WIN, BY FEARING TO ATTEMPT.

If you have faith as small as a mustard seed, you can say to this mountain, "Move…" and it will move.

Matthew 17:20

151

A GOOD REPUTATION IS MORE VALUABLE THAN MONEY.

A good name is rather to be chosen than great riches.
Proverbs 22:1 KJV

THERE ARE MANY THINGS THAT ARE
ESSENTIAL TO ARRIVING AT TRUE
PEACE OF MIND, AND ONE OF THE
MOST IMPORTANT IS FAITH,
WHICH CANNOT BE ACQUIRED
WITHOUT PRAYER.

*Whatever you ask for in prayer, believe that you have
received it, and it will be yours.*

Mark 11:24

153

PATIENCE IS BITTER, BUT ITS FRUIT IS SWEET.

You need to keep on patiently doing God's will if you want him to do for you all that he has promised.
Hebrews 10:36 TLB

154

THE COURSE OF HUMAN HISTORY
IS DETERMINED, NOT BY WHAT
HAPPENS IN THE SKIES, BUT
BY WHAT TAKES PLACE
IN OUR HEARTS.

Keep my words and store up my commands within you ...
write them on the tablet of your heart.

Proverbs 7:1,3

CLASS OF
2000

155

ANYONE CAN DO HIS BEST. GOD HELPS US DO BETTER THAN OUR BEST.

Now glory be to God who by his mighty power at work within us is able to do far more than we would ever dare to ask or even dream of.
Ephesians 3:20 TLB

156

THIS ABOVE ALL: TO THINE OWN
SELF BE TRUE, AND IT MUST
FOLLOW, AS THE NIGHT THE DAY,
THOU CANST NOT THEN
BE FALSE TO ANY MAN.

You deserve honesty from the heart; yes,
utter sincerity and truthfulness. Oh, give me this wisdom.
Psalm 51:6 TLB

Acknowledgements

We acknowledge and thank the following people for the quotes used in this book: Charles R. Swindoll (4), Roger Von Oech (5), William James (6), Ernest Hemingway (7), Charles Spurgeon (8), Margaret Bonnano (9), Mark Twain (10,59), Henry Ford (11), Martin Luther (13), Aldous Huxley (14), Johann Wolfgang von Goethe (16,17), Louis D. Brandels (18), Miguel de Cervantes (20), Franklin Delano Roosevelt (21,38), Michel de Montaigne (22,75), Alexander Graham Bell (23), Keshavan Nair (24), Robert Browning (25), Arnold Glasgow (27), Euripides (28), Robert G. Ingersoll (29), Marcus Aurelius Antoninus (30), Charlotte Bronte (31), Helen Keller (32), Peter Marshall (33), Richard Bach (34), Dale Carnegie (35), Victor Hugo (36), James Thurber (37), Rachael Carson (39), Confucius (40), William Shedd (42), Heraclitus (43), Alexander Pope (45), Daniel Webster (46), William Makepeace Thackeray (47), Soren Kierkegaard (48), Jonathan Swift (49), Henry Wadsworth Longfellow (50,82), Diane Sawyer (52), Tennessee Williams (53), Grantland Rice (54), Martha Washington (55), Booker T. Washington (56), Andrew Jackson (57), Dorothy Dix (58), Say (60), Benjamin Franklin (61), P.J. Bailey (62), Aristotle (63), Eleanor Roosevelt (64), Edmund Burke (65), T.S. Eliot (66), Virgil (67), Emily Bronte (68), Horace (69,110), Julia Carney (70), Theodore Roosevelt (71), Jean de La Fontaine (73), Gary Smalley and John Trent (74), Sir Walter Scott (76), Les Brown (77), Suetonius (78), John D. Rockefeller, Jr. (80), Robert C. Edward (82), C.F. Richardson (83), Fanny J. Crosby (84), Amy Carmichael (85), Kin Hubbard (86), Robert Louis Stevenson (87), Frances Ridley Havergal (88), John A. Shedd (89), A.W. Tozer (90), Ralph Waldo Emerson (92,96), Thomas Fuller (93), Abraham Lincoln (94), Alexander Maclaren (97), F.B. Meyer (98),

Ruth E. Renkel (99), Descartes (100), Katherine Graham (102), Alfred Lord Tennyson (103), John Sculley (104), Aristotle (105), Dorthea Brande (106), Mary Bryant (107), Charles H. Spurgeon (108), Homer (109), Charles A. Lindbergh (111), Norman Macleod (112), Lewis Morris (113), Ovid (114), Bacon (115), Ambrose Redmoon (116), Jean Francois Regnard (117), Louis D. Brandeis (118), Thomas Carlyle (120,146), Steven Pagent (121), Anthony J. d'Angelo (122), Albert Einstein (124), Winifred Newman (125), P.K. Shaw (126), E.W. Scripps (127), Charlotte Elliott (131), Dante (138), Corrie ten Boom (139), William Carey (140), Lucius C. Lactantuis (141), William Blake (142), Mahatma Gandhi (143), Saint Thomas Acquinas (144), Saint Bernard (145), W.E.B. Du Bois (147), Jefferson Davis (148), Lady Bird Johnson (149), William M. Evarts (150), Shakespeare (151,157), Raymond Holliwell (152), John Wooden (153), Pietro Aretino (154), Sir Arthur Kent (155), Andrew Young (156).

Additional copies of this book
and other titles from Honor Books are available
from your local bookstore.

God's Little Instruction Book
God's Little Instruction Book for Parents
God's Little Instruction Book for Leaders

If you have enjoyed this book or it has
impacted your life, we would like to hear from you.
Please contact us at:

Honor Books
Department E
P.O. Box 55388
Tulsa, Oklahoma 74155